How to Make Money in the Metaverse

Top 10 Ways to Earn Passive Income in Virtual Worlds — Even Without Coding or Tech Skills

By Joe Cor

Published by Live Stronger Faster

This book is for educational and informational purposes only. The author and publisher are not engaged in rendering legal, financial, or other professional advice. Readers should consult a qualified professional before making any financial decisions.

First Edition

Table of Contents

Introduction

The metaverse is no longer just a futuristic concept or a playground for gamers. It has rapidly become one of the most innovative economic frontiers of the 21st century—an expanding network of interconnected virtual worlds where real businesses are built, real value is exchanged, and real income is earned. This book is designed to open the doors to those opportunities. Whether you're a complete beginner or someone who has dabbled in Web3, here you'll discover practical, accessible, and proven ways to generate passive income in the metaverse—methods that do not require you to code, have advanced technology, or even understand crypto at an expert level. You are entering an economy built on creativity, ownership, digital labor, and decentralized markets, and for the first time in history, beginners can carve out a place inside it just as effectively as seasoned professionals.

We are living through a moment where the virtual economy is expanding faster than many traditional industries. Brands, celebrities, entrepreneurs, and investors are staking digital claims in virtual real estate, virtual stores, NFT-based product lines, avatar fashion, metaverse courses, social clubs, play-to-earn gaming ecosystems, and virtual event spaces. Income generation in this digital frontier mirrors the real world in many ways—there are jobs, rentals, services, and businesses—but with one key difference: scale. In the metaverse, your audience is not limited to your city or country. You can build something once and monetize it across continents, time zones, and cultures without needing physical inventory, shipping logistics, or a marketing budget equivalent to large corporations. The metaverse rewards creativity, timing, and understanding how digital ecosystems work.

This book begins with a simple truth: earning money in the metaverse does **not** require a massive investment. In fact, many people start with nothing but a laptop, a smartphone, and a little curiosity. Thousands of creators earn income by designing avatar clothing, building simple 3D scenes using no-code tools, hosting virtual workshops, or participating in play-to-earn economies. Others rent out digital land, flip NFTs, host sponsored events, or build micro-businesses that operate entirely in virtual worlds. For some, these streams become side income; for others, they grow into full-time businesses that far exceed what they ever imagined possible. The metaverse removes traditional barriers: no landlord gatekeeping your store location, no need to stock physical inventory, no need for offices, employees, or even deep pockets. What you need is strategy—and that is exactly what this book provides. The reason “passive income” in the metaverse has become such a powerful concept is because digital assets can continue producing revenue long after they are created. A virtual store can sell items 24/7, even while you sleep. A digital real estate parcel can be rented to event organizers, creators, or advertisers on a recurring basis. An NFT collection can generate resale royalties every time it changes hands. A simple metaverse experience—such as a mini-game, meditation space, art gallery, or digital classroom—can attract sponsorships, partnerships, or paid visitors without requiring constant labor. This shift toward automated, scalable, and borderless income is what makes the metaverse so unique. You are not exchanging hours for dollars—you are creating value that multiplies across digital ecosystems.

But before you can profit, you must understand the underlying structure of the metaverse economy. It is built on three pillars: **digital ownership**, **digital identity**, and **digital experiences**. Ownership is enabled by blockchain and NFTs, giving you provable, transferable control over digital items. Identity is expressed through customizable avatars, profiles, and reputations that carry across virtual worlds. Experiences—events, games, shops, clubs, concerts, workplaces—are where economic activity actually happens. When you understand how these pillars interact, you understand where the money flows. And once you understand where the money flows, you can strategically position yourself to earn from it. This book will take you through the top ten ways to earn passive income in the metaverse—not theories, but practical pathways that anyone can follow. You will learn how virtual real estate works and how people rent billboards, buildings, or land for profit. You will learn how creators design wearable items, avatar skins, or digital collectibles that sell for recurring revenue. You will see how educators, coaches, and influencers build virtual classrooms or meeting spaces that attract paying audiences. You will discover how play-to-earn games reward players with crypto or digital assets they can resell. You will even explore the rise of decentralized jobs, freelancing opportunities, and investment strategies that operate completely inside the metaverse. Each method is broken down into beginner steps, technical requirements, startup costs, and monetization tips, giving you a clear roadmap from idea to income.

What makes this book different is its focus on accessibility. The metaverse can appear complex or overwhelming to someone who is new, filled with unfamiliar terminology and fast-changing platforms. But behind all of the technical language is a simple idea: the metaverse is just a new version of the internet—one that is more immersive, more social, and more economically open. You don't need to understand every blockchain protocol, every NFT standard, or every game engine to succeed. You only need to learn where you can add value, what types of digital assets people pay for, and how to position yourself inside virtual ecosystems. The goal of this introduction is not to impress you with jargon—it is to empower you with clarity, confidence, and the knowledge that you can participate meaningfully in this new frontier.

You are also entering this space at a critical moment. The early adopters have already planted their flags—some have made fortunes, others have made mistakes. But the next wave of growth is where the most opportunity will exist. Major corporations are investing billions into virtual infrastructure. Educational institutions are launching courses in digital worlds. Real estate firms are opening virtual offices. Fashion houses are releasing exclusive digital-only collections. Musicians are performing metaverse concerts with millions of virtual attendees. And entrepreneurs—just like you—are transforming simple ideas into profitable ventures using tools that didn't exist a decade ago. This is the kind of technological shift that happens only a few times in a generation, and those who understand it first are the ones who benefit most.

More importantly, you must see yourself not as a passive observer but as a participant in a growing digital economy. In the same way the early days of the internet rewarded those who built websites, blogs, YouTube channels, and e-commerce stores, the metaverse will reward those who take action early.

The people who learn how digital land works will own valuable property. The people who design digital goods will supply the demand for avatar identity. The people who create virtual experiences will become the hosts, educators, entertainers, and leaders of this new world. And the people who understand how Web3's decentralized infrastructure works will shape the future of online income itself.

As you move through this book, you will notice a recurring theme: simplicity. Every chapter is crafted to help you take achievable steps, regardless of experience level. You will learn not only what to do but why it works, who is already succeeding with these methods, and how you can replicate their results. You will gain a toolkit of strategies—some fast and low-cost, others long-term and scalable—that allow you to diversify your income and carve out your own place in the metaverse economy. By the time you finish, you will have a clear understanding of how to earn passive income in virtual worlds and how to build a digital empire that can grow with you over time.

Welcome to **Book 4: How to Make Money in the Metaverse**. You are stepping into a world where imagination becomes income, creativity becomes currency, and the opportunities are as limitless as the virtual universe itself. Get ready to learn, to build, and to profit. Your journey into the new digital economy begins now.

Chapter 1

Understanding Metaverse Economics

To succeed in the metaverse, you must first understand how its economy works. Unlike traditional economies, which depend on physical infrastructure such as land, buildings, transportation, and local currency systems, the metaverse economy is built entirely on digital foundations. These foundations include blockchain-based ownership, digital identities connected to avatars, decentralized marketplaces for goods and services, and a network of interconnected virtual worlds where value can flow freely across platforms. Whether you plan to become an investor, creator, gamer, educator, or entrepreneur, your income inside the metaverse will be shaped by your ability to understand where value originates, how it moves, and how people exchange it.

The core idea is simple: in the metaverse, value is created through **digital scarcity**, **experiential demand**, and **virtual identity**. Digital scarcity refers to assets that exist in limited quantities—land parcels, rare NFTs, wearable items, or exclusive access passes. Although these items are digital, blockchain technology makes them provably limited. Experiential demand refers to the appetite people have for immersive environments like virtual concerts, classrooms, events, games, and businesses. Virtual identity refers to the way people present themselves through avatar customization, digital fashion, social reputation, and online status. These three elements—scarcity, experience, and identity—form the economic engine that powers nearly every earning opportunity.

To understand metaverse economics at a deeper level, you must look at the difference between **Web2 economies** and **Web3/metaverse economies**. In Web2—traditional apps like Instagram, YouTube, or Fortnite—users can buy digital items, but they don't truly own them. A Fortnite skin cannot be sold or transferred. An Instagram account cannot be moved to another platform. A YouTube video cannot generate value outside of YouTube. But in Web3, ownership becomes portable. If you buy a wearable item in a metaverse world that runs on an open standard, you may use, sell, rent, or transfer it across compatible platforms. This creates the first real digital economy where you—not a corporation—control your assets.

Understanding **ownership** is essential because ownership creates passive income. When you own a digital asset, such as a virtual property, a piece of land, or a unique NFT that provides access or utilities, you can monetize it repeatedly. You can rent it, resell it, license it, lease it, advertise on it, or bundle it with other digital goods. Ownership unlocks monetization pathways that are impossible in closed platforms like traditional video games. This shift is why so many investors and entrepreneurs are flocking to Web3—it's the biggest shift in digital economics since the creation of the internet itself.

The second major component of the metaverse economy is **interoperability**, which refers to the ability for assets, identities, and experiences to move between different virtual worlds. Although full interoperability is still developing, the trend is clear: future metaverse platforms will be connected like today's websites are connected through the internet. As a creator or investor, this means your digital goods and virtual assets may eventually work across multiple ecosystems, increasing demand and long-term value. Think of it as owning a piece of land that exists in several worlds at once—a powerful concept that will shape future income opportunities.

Another foundational idea is **token-based economies**, where cryptocurrency tokens represent in-game money, governance rights, rewards, or ownership stakes in virtual ecosystems. These tokens often fluctuate in value based on demand, scarcity, and utility. Understanding tokenomics—how tokens are created, distributed, and used—is essential for anyone who wants to invest in or build inside the metaverse. Tokens can be earned through gameplay, staking digital assets, contributing to decentralized platforms, providing liquidity, or participating in community governance. In many play-to-earn economies, tokens serve as both rewards and tradable currency, allowing players to convert digital time and skill into real-world income.

Next, you must understand **supply and demand** inside virtual worlds. Just like the physical world, the metaverse has limited prime real estate locations, high-demand fashion items, popular event venues, and scarce collectible items. Some areas inside worlds like Decentraland or The Sandbox attract heavy traffic and therefore carry higher rental or sale value. Avatar fashion brands release limited-edition wearables that command premium prices. Events, concerts, and festivals require rented virtual land or stages, fueling demand for well-designed spaces. Digital scarcity doesn't happen by accident—it is intentionally created to mirror the tension between supply and demand in the physical world, making metaverse assets function like traditional commodities.

Another important part of metaverse economics is **creator-driven value**. Unlike physical economies, where manufacturing requires factories, materials, and distribution channels, in the metaverse a single creator can build a digital asset using free or low-cost tools and sell it repeatedly to thousands of buyers. For example, a designer can create a wearable jacket for avatars using a free 3D modeling tool and sell it in a marketplace like Decentraland or Roblox. A builder can design a virtual home and sell it as a template. A musician can mint a song as an NFT and include special perks or access rights. Digital creation has near-zero marginal cost, meaning creators can scale their businesses infinitely without increasing overhead.

Finally, you must understand **user behavior**. People enter virtual worlds for three reasons: entertainment, expression, and opportunity. Entertainment includes gaming, concerts, social events, and interactive experiences. Expression includes customizing avatars, purchasing fashion items, decorating virtual homes, and building social status inside communities. Opportunity includes entrepreneurship, investment, education, networking, and skill development. Every profitable business or income stream inside the metaverse is built around serving one or more of these motivations. If you understand why people spend money in virtual worlds, you can design digital assets, services, and experiences that meet those needs.

When you combine all of these elements—ownership, identity, scarcity, interoperability, tokenomics, creator value, and user motivation—you gain a complete blueprint for understanding the metaverse economy. It is a digital environment where creativity meets technology, where scarcity meets demand, and where individuals have more economic power than in any previous digital ecosystem. The metaverse is not a trend; it is the next evolution of online value creation. You are early, and that gives you an extraordinary advantage. Before you learn specific income strategies, you must internalize these economic fundamentals. Once you do, every opportunity described in this book will make sense, and you will be ready to profit from one of the most transformative economic revolutions of our time.

The Architect of the Neon District

Aiden Navarro had never considered himself an early adopter of anything. He had always admired technology from a safe distance, watching others take risks while he stuck to routines that felt familiar and predictable. But after losing his job during a restructuring that blindsided the entire company, Aiden found himself searching the internet late at night, looking for something—anything—that could offer a new beginning. One night, a video thumbnail caught his attention: *"How People Are Earning Real Income in the Metaverse."* Curious and with nothing left to lose, he clicked.

The video showed digital landscapes glowing with neon lights, avatar-run businesses, bustling marketplaces, and creators selling items that didn't physically exist but generated very real money. People were building homes, shops, art galleries, fashion brands, and even entire neighborhoods in worlds he had never heard of. At first, Aiden assumed it was exaggerated marketing, but the comments told a different story. Thousands of people shared their earnings, their mistakes, their wins, and their growth. Something clicked inside him—not excitement, but possibility.

Aiden downloaded one of the metaverse platforms, created a simple avatar, and stepped into a city called the Neon District. Towering holographic billboards hovered over the streets. Avatars strolled past digital cafes, art installations, and clothing shops. A group of musicians performed live in a floating concert bubble. Everything felt surreal, yet strangely logical. He walked into a virtual plaza where creators were showcasing assets—virtual furniture, digital clothing, customizable spaces, and 3D models that could be purchased or downloaded. Aiden didn't know what any of this meant yet, but he could feel the energy of a thriving economy.

As he wandered, he met an avatar named Liora, a creator who designed virtual buildings. She had made a full-time income selling templates—simple digital structures like lofts, offices, and galleries. "Once you understand metaverse economics," she told him, "it's just like building anything in the real world...but the scale is unlimited." She explained digital scarcity, token-based ownership, avatar identity, and the power of creator-driven value. Aiden listened as she spoke about renting virtual land to brands hosting events, selling wearable fashion items in limited editions, and designing immersive environments for clients around the world.

Liora invited him to her workshop. Inside, she opened panels showing how she built and sold her digital structures. "This loft design?" she said. "I made it six months ago. It's still selling every week. I don't have to rebuild it, package it, or ship it. Digital assets work for you long after you create them." Aiden watched, fascinated, as she navigated through a 3D modeling interface, explained tokenomics, and showed how ownership worked through blockchain. The more she taught him, the more Aiden realized that the metaverse economy didn't favor the rich or educated—it favored the imaginative.

He decided to try. Aiden found free tutorials, joined creator communities, and spent hours learning the basics of building digital structures. His first attempts were rough. His walls floated, his doors didn't line up, and his textures looked like melted plastic. But creators encouraged him, gave feedback, and reminded him that every successful designer started clumsy. Piece by piece, he got better. He built a simple, modern studio with glowing accents inspired by the Neon

District. He uploaded it to the marketplace, set a modest price, and went to sleep unsure if anyone would ever see it.

The next morning, he woke up to a notification: *"You've made your first sale."* Aiden stared at the screen, unsure if it was a glitch. But it wasn't—someone had bought his digital studio. His heart raced. That single sale—small as it was—felt like a turning point in his life. For the first time since losing his job, he felt hope.

Weeks passed. Aiden refined his designs, expanded his catalog, and even collaborated with Liora on a new district inside the platform. His work gained recognition, and he was soon invited to submit designs for a major virtual festival. His Neon District-inspired architecture became iconic, attracting brands, creators, and social hangout groups. One day, as he stood in his virtual gallery watching dozens of avatars explore his latest collection, he realized something profound: he wasn't just surviving; he was thriving in an economy he had once believed was only for tech geniuses.

Aiden Navarro, once a laid-off employee unsure of his future, had become known as *The Architect of the Neon District*. His virtual assets generated passive income around the clock. His creations shaped the skyline of a world that existed only in code and imagination. And every day, as new avatars walked past the glowing buildings he designed, Aiden smiled knowing that he had discovered not just a new economy—but a new version of himself.

Chapter 2

The Top Passive Income Streams in the Metaverse

Passive income in the metaverse is fundamentally different from passive income in the physical world. In the physical world, passive income often requires substantial upfront investment—real estate purchases, large stock portfolios, or high capital ventures. In the metaverse, however, passive income is driven by digital assets, digital ownership, and automated systems that can generate revenue continuously with minimal ongoing effort. Because these virtual environments operate 24 hours a day, attracting global audiences across time zones, your work can earn money even when you are offline. To fully benefit from these opportunities, you must understand the primary categories of passive income that consistently generate revenue inside virtual worlds.

One of the most popular forms of passive income is **virtual real estate renting**. Inside metaverse platforms like Decentraland, The Sandbox, Spatial, and emerging immersive worlds, virtual landowners have the ability to rent plots to brands, event organizers, creators, and gamers. This is very similar to physical property rentals; the difference is that virtual land requires no physical maintenance, no repairs, no utilities, and no furniture. Once you own a digital parcel, you can monetize it indefinitely by leasing it out to users who wish to build stores, offices, galleries, festival grounds, or social hubs. Rental prices vary depending on the platform, the location within the world, and the popularity of nearby areas. Parcels near high-traffic plazas, teleportation points, or major event hubs often command premium rents. For individuals seeking passive income, virtual land rentals offer a consistent revenue stream without ongoing labor.

Another high-demand passive income stream is **wearable or avatar fashion sales**, especially when designed as limited-edition items. Avatar identity is one of the strongest economic drivers inside virtual worlds. People want to express themselves, show status, or stand out visually, and they are willing to pay for digital clothing, accessories, and skins. The beauty of wearable sales is that once you create a digital fashion item, you can sell it repeatedly without producing new inventory. Marketplace platforms automate sales, distribution, and royalty payments. Many creators also incorporate scarcity by releasing limited quantities or special seasonal collections. This scarcity increases value and demand, allowing creators to earn passive royalties for months or years after launch.

NFT royalty income is another major component of metaverse passive earnings. When you mint NFTs—whether they represent art, music, digital collectibles, memberships, or in-game items—you can set a royalty percentage that pays you automatically each time the asset is resold. This means that your creation continues generating revenue long after the initial sale, especially if it becomes popular within the community. Artists, musicians, and developers have used this model to build recurring income streams that function like intellectual property royalties. As long as trading continues, you continue earning without lifting a finger.

A rapidly growing passive income stream is **play-to-earn staking and yield farming**, where users lock digital tokens or NFTs into blockchain-based systems that reward them with additional tokens over time. Many metaverse platforms integrate DeFi (decentralized finance) elements, allowing users to stake land, stake assets, or participate in liquidity pools tied to the native ecosystem. These rewards accumulate passively based on platform activity, token supply, and staking duration. Staking can provide stable returns if managed correctly, though it does require understanding tokenomics, market conditions, and platform reliability.

Next is **operating virtual billboards or advertising spaces**, which function similarly to renting advertising space in a real city. High-traffic virtual locations—intersections, plazas, teleportation zones, or popular event districts—attract brands looking to promote events, product launches, or experiences. If you own a billboard or a structure with visible space, you can lease that advertising space for passive monthly income. Some people create multi-panel billboards and rent each section separately for additional revenue. This model mirrors physical advertising, but with significantly lower overhead and global visibility.

Another in-demand way to earn passive income is **creating and selling templates or modular assets**. Builders often design digital structures—homes, offices, clubs, galleries, stages, lounges, or shops—and sell them as ready-to-use templates. Because users can purchase the design and deploy it instantly, templates are extremely popular among beginners who want a quick way to set up virtual spaces. A single template can be sold thousands of times across multiple marketplaces, creating long-term recurring revenue. Templates require only the upfront time required to design them; after that, marketplaces handle transactions automatically, producing ongoing passive income.

One of the most innovative passive income methods is **running automated experiences**, such as AI-powered NPCs (non-player characters), guided tours, self-paced games, meditation rooms, or learning environments. After building the experience once, you can monetize through entry fees, memberships, sponsorships, or in-game purchases. Automated experiences work continuously without supervision, generating revenue from visitors around the world. This model is especially powerful in platforms that support persistent environments where experiences stay active even when the creator is offline.

There is also growing opportunity in **music and sound design licensing**, where creators upload ambient loops, soundtracks, sound effects, or background audio that other builders can integrate into their environments. Because sound plays a critical role in immersion, audio assets are in constant demand. Once uploaded to a marketplace, these tracks can generate long-term passive income as creators purchase licenses for use in their worlds.

Another passive income pathway is **membership NFTs**, where holders receive ongoing access to exclusive spaces, content, or privileges. Membership NFTs can include premium clubs, private communities, metaverse mastermind groups, gated live events, or VIP-only areas. Members pay initially for the NFT, and creator income continues through royalty fees each time the membership is sold or transferred. This model is similar to subscription businesses, but powered by blockchain automation.

Finally, one of the simplest and most beginner-friendly passive income options is **reselling digital goods through affiliate programs or marketplace revenue shares**, where creators earn a percentage of sales made through their referral links. Some metaverse platforms pay commissions for new user signups, land purchases, event registrations, wearable sales, or NFT marketplace activity. Beginners without technical skills can monetize simply by promoting virtual assets they enjoy using.

When you understand these passive income streams—land renting, wearable sales, NFT royalties, staking, advertising, templates, automated experiences, sound licensing, membership NFTs, and affiliate income—you gain a solid foundation for earning within the metaverse economy. Each method has its own learning curve, startup cost, and long-term potential, but all share one common advantage: scalability. While physical businesses require physical presence, virtual income streams can scale across millions of users with no inventory, no shipping, and no traditional overhead. The metaverse rewards creativity, timing, and vision. Once you choose your path, build strategically, and position yourself correctly, passive income becomes both achievable and sustainable.

The Marketplace of Endless Doors

Maya Ortez had always been fascinated by the idea of passive income, but every attempt she made in the real world felt impossible. Rentals required credit and capital she didn't have. Side businesses demanded time she couldn't spare. Stocks felt unpredictable, and she didn't have the confidence to invest without fear. But everything changed the day she walked through a shimmering doorway inside a virtual world known as Aurora City.

The city pulsed with energy—holograms floated above shops, neon-lit walkways stretched across the skyline, and glowing signs advertised everything from virtual concerts to meditation zones to avatar nightclubs. It felt like a dream made real through pixels. Maya, who had entered Aurora City out of curiosity, found herself standing in the heart of a marketplace known as The Bazaar of Endless Doors. Each door radiated with its own color and texture, each leading to a different income opportunity.

A guide appeared beside her—a tall avatar dressed in obsidian robes, with a voice that resonated like a calm echo. "Welcome, seeker," the guide said. "I am Solara, keeper of the Bazaar. Each door represents a path to earning inside this world. You may explore them freely." Maya nodded nervously. She had never created anything digital before. She didn't know how to model 3D items or design NFTs. But something inside her urged her to continue.

The first door she opened glowed gold. Inside was a panoramic view of floating islands dotted with structures. "This is the Land of Rentals," Solara explained. Maya watched avatars renting plots for shops, galleries, and event venues. She saw contracts being signed with a click, and parcels being leased with no physical maintenance. It felt unreal, yet the numbers hovering above each land plot reflected real payments. "People pay for visibility," Solara said. "They pay for space. They pay for foot traffic. Just like the physical world, but without the limitations."

The second door pulsed with cobalt blue light. Inside, avatars strutted along a digital runway wearing vivid, shimmering outfits. "Wearables," Solara said with a smile. "Digitally crafted fashion." Maya watched as creators sold jackets, wings, dresses, masks, and glowing accessories—some simple, some breathtakingly complex. She saw limited-edition drops selling out within minutes. She saw creators minting items that generated royalties each time they changed hands. "Identity powers this world," Solara whispered. "Help someone express themselves, and you help yourself earn."

The next door revealed an art gallery filled with ever-changing frames. Each time an avatar purchased a piece, the artwork teleported to their inventory while a small royalty flowed back to its creator. "NFT royalties," Solara said. "Create once, earn forever." Maya felt a spark of excitement. She didn't need to be an expert to contribute—she simply needed to understand what people loved.

She walked through door after door. A radiant purple door led to a room filled with glowing tokens—staking pools humming with energy. Another door opened to a courtyard where billboards towered above avatar crowds, rented out to brands and performers. The next led to a workshop of templates and modular buildings that sold repeatedly to users eager to launch their own virtual spaces. Still another revealed automated experiences: AI-driven tours, interactive puzzles, and meditation sanctuaries where visitors paid small entry fees, generating continuous revenue for their creators.

Maya finally stopped at a small emerald-green door near the edge of the bazaar. Inside was a quiet music studio where creators uploaded soundtracks that others licensed for their virtual spaces. Gentle ambient music played as she watched avatars preview audio clips. "Sound shapes emotion," Solara said softly. "And emotion shapes experience. Every builder needs audio. Every world needs mood." For the first time,

Maya felt something she hadn't felt in years: possibility. She realized she didn't have to master every door—she only needed to choose one. The metaverse wasn't asking her to become a technical expert; it was offering her a chance to participate, to experiment, to create something that could grow even while she slept.

She turned to Solara. "Which door should I choose?" she asked. Solara's avatar smiled, her eyes reflecting the colors of the marketplace. "Choose the door that excites you," she said. "The one that feels like play, not work. Passive income begins with passion."

Maya looked back at the emerald-green door. She loved music. She always had. Even as a child, she recorded little melodies on her phone, dreaming of one day creating soundtracks for movies or games. The realization hit her like a rush of wind: she could start here, with sound. Simple loops. Atmospheric tracks. Relaxing backgrounds. Something that felt like her.

"I choose this one," she said, touching the emerald frame.

As her finger made contact, the door pulsed with a warm glow, accepting her choice. "Then step forward," Solara said, her voice echoing softly. "Begin your journey. This world rewards those who dare to create."

Maya stepped through the doorway into her new beginning—a world where passive income wasn't a distant dream, but an open invitation. And as she began crafting her first sound loop, she realized something profound: in the metaverse, every creator starts at zero, but none have to stay there. The doors were endless. The opportunities limitless. And now, she had chosen hers.

Chapter 3

How Digital Real Estate Really Works in the Metaverse

Digital real estate is one of the most exciting and profitable opportunities inside the metaverse, but it is also the one most misunderstood by beginners. To fully profit from this category of passive income, you must understand what metaverse real estate actually is, why it carries real monetary value, and how you can strategically invest, rent, flip, or build on it. Unlike physical real estate, digital land doesn't exist in the traditional sense—there is no physical dimension, soil, construction, or geography. Instead, digital real estate refers to **virtual land parcels** inside specific metaverse platforms. Each parcel is a unique coordinate within that world's map, represented by an NFT. The owner of that parcel has control over what is built on it, who can visit it, and how it is monetized. Ownership is verifiable through blockchain technology, ensuring scarcity, transferability, and security.

The first concept to understand is **platform-based value**. Not all digital land is created equal. Each metaverse operates like a separate country, with its own culture, economy, population density, development style, and long-term growth potential. A parcel in Decentraland functions differently than one in The Sandbox, Roblox, Meta Horizon Worlds, Spatial, or emerging decentralized worlds. When evaluating land value, you must first assess the ecosystem: How many active users does the platform have? How fast is the world growing? What type of users does it attract—brands, gamers, creators, investors, educators, or a mix? A world with higher activity and more commercial development often results in higher land appreciation, higher rental demand, and stronger traffic for businesses built on parcels.

The second concept is **location inside the world**, which is one of the most powerful pricing factors. Digital geography follows real-world logic in surprising ways. Parcels near central plazas, portals, spawn points, transportation hubs, event districts, and brand-owned properties typically command premium pricing. These high-traffic areas attract visitors naturally, making them especially valuable for income-generating projects such as shops, galleries, clubs, event venues, and advertising billboards. Just like major cities in real life, digital cities develop "hot spots" where foot traffic is concentrated. Smart investors look for parcels near key landmarks, upcoming development zones, or areas where major projects are planned.

The third concept is **utility**, which refers to what you can actually do with your land. Utility determines monetization. A parcel can be used to host events, rent to creators, build an NFT gallery, create a virtual office, launch a game, run a training center, or operate a retail store. Land with higher flexibility tends to have higher value. Some worlds allow full 3D building freedom, while others restrict building size, function, or theme. When purchasing land, always check: What can be built? What tools or builders are supported? Are there limitations on height, style, or commercial activity? Worlds that support enterprise-level tools and developer-friendly structures create stronger long-term value.

You must also understand **supply and scarcity**. Digital land is valuable because it is finite—platforms issue a fixed number of parcels, preventing new land from being created later. This scarcity mimics real estate economics but without the physical constraints. Because land supply is fixed and user populations can grow infinitely, long-term demand is structurally designed to rise. This is one reason early investors in Decentraland and The Sandbox saw dramatic appreciation during the first metaverse boom. Although prices fluctuate with broader crypto markets, scarcity ensures that prime parcels retain long-term relevance.

The next principle is **market timing**. Buying land early in the lifecycle of a metaverse can yield massive returns if the platform gains popularity. However, late-stage worlds with established traffic provide more predictable income and safer rentals. The key is understanding your strategy. If you want long-term holding and appreciation, earlier-stage projects may suit you. If you want immediate rental income, choose mature worlds with existing foot traffic. Always evaluate platform roadmaps, development updates, ecosystem partnerships, and user growth when determining timing.

Now we move into monetization strategies. The most beginner-friendly method is **land renting**, where you lease your parcel to creators, brands, or event organizers. Rental income can be weekly, monthly, or tied to specific events. Creators rent land to build galleries, schools, stores, or clubs. Brands rent land for virtual activations, product launches, or ad campaigns. Festivals and conferences rent land for temporary builds. Because renters cover build costs, landowners earn entirely passive income without additional effort.

Another strategy is **building and flipping**, where you purchase land, develop a high-quality structure, and then resell it at a higher price. This mirrors real-world house flipping but with significantly lower cost and shorter project timelines. A well-designed art gallery, club, office, or mansion can dramatically increase the land's value. Buyers often prefer turnkey developed parcels instead of building from scratch. A strong aesthetic, functional layout, and high-traffic location help maximize resale value.

The third income method is **event monetization**, where you use land to host concerts, workshops, meetups, fashion shows, game tournaments, educational classes, or product launches. You can charge entry fees, sell VIP passes, offer sponsorship opportunities, or sell in-event digital goods. Event monetization works best when your land is located near a central hub, but well-designed private venues can also attract high demand.

Another popular approach is **business deployment**, where you build a fully functional virtual business—such as a store, mini-game, training center, studio, or gallery—that generates consistent sales. Marketplace-integrated worlds allow you to sell items directly from your land, making each visitor a potential customer. Businesses that offer ongoing value—education, entertainment, social experiences, or exclusive merchandise—can produce recurring income with minimal upkeep.

Digital land also enables **advertising-based monetization**. If your parcel is located in a high-traffic area, brands may pay to place ads, billboards, holographic posters, or product displays. Some landowners earn more from advertising than rentals, especially during major metaverse events. This method works particularly well when you own structures with large and visible surfaces.

Lastly, landowners can build **virtual neighborhoods or districts**, where multiple plots are transformed into a cohesive themed area—fashion districts, art blocks, gaming neighborhoods, educational campuses, or wellness retreats. Districts create immersive destinations, attracting visitors and businesses. They can be monetized through leasing, sponsorships, tourism, events, or branded partnerships.

Understanding digital real estate requires a shift in perspective. You are not buying "land" in the traditional sense—you are buying attention, access, placement, visibility, and creative freedom within a digital economy. When you approach land the way digital entrepreneurs approach websites—for traffic, conversions, experience, and monetization—you begin to see how real and powerful this opportunity is. Digital real estate is one of the strongest cornerstones of metaverse wealth because it connects creativity, ownership, and audience demand. Once you master how it works, you unlock one of the most scalable income engines in the entire virtual economy.

The Parcel Above the Moonlit River

Rina Kuroda never expected a single piece of digital land to change her life. She had signed into the metaverse out of curiosity, wandering through floating cities, neon markets, and virtual gardens just to escape the stress of her corporate job. One night, she stumbled upon a place called the Moonlit River District—a shimmering expanse of glowing water that reflected the constellations of a virtual sky. Bridges arched gracefully across the water, and glowing lanterns drifted along the river's surface. It felt peaceful in a way the real world rarely did.

As she explored, she noticed a small parcel of land perched above the river, overlooking the water from a high cliff. A hologram hovered above it: *For Sale — 28,000 Credits.* Rina laughed at first. Why would anyone pay for digital dirt suspended in a world made of code? She almost walked away—until an older avatar approached her.

"You're looking at one of the best views in this world," he said. His name floated above his head: TORIN. He wore a simple robe, and his avatar had a serene, knowing expression. "Views matter," he continued. "Even in digital worlds. People pay for places that make them feel something."

Rina raised an eyebrow. "It's not real."

Torin smiled. “Neither are emotions. But we still feel them.”

He explained how digital real estate worked—the scarcity, the utility, the ability to build anything she imagined. He showed her nearby parcels that had transformed into thriving businesses. A glowing bridge café that sold virtual pastries. A riverside art gallery hosting weekly exhibitions. A meditation dome where visitors floated in zero gravity while listening to ambient music.

“These parcels earn money every day,” Torin said. “Some from rent, some from events, some from simple foot traffic. People aren’t paying for land… they’re paying for an experience.”

Rina stood in silence, staring out over the shimmering river. She felt the same calm she’d felt the first time she found this place. Without fully understanding why, she bought the parcel.

At first, she didn’t know what to build. She wasn’t a creator, designer, or entrepreneur. She worked in a corporate office, spending her days in spreadsheets and meetings. The idea of building something from scratch terrified her. But each evening after work, she returned to her parcel, letting the glow of the river inspire her.

She found free tutorials, watched builders create beautiful spaces, and learned the basics of shaping structures from voxels and polygons. Her first attempts were lopsided, but piece by piece, she constructed a small circular pavilion made of translucent panels that reflected the moonlight. She filled the interior with cushions, lanterns, and soft ambient music. It felt like a sanctuary—her sanctuary.

One night, as she adjusted the final lantern, an avatar suddenly entered. “This place is incredible,” the stranger said softly. Rina felt shy but grateful. The avatar sat, listened to the music, and then purchased a virtual drink from the small vending pod she had added as an experiment. The next day, five more avatars visited. Then twenty. Some meditated silently. Others brought friends. Within a week, her pavilion—now named *The Moonlight Sanctuary*—became a popular relaxation spot.

But the real surprise came when event organizers reached out asking to rent the space for guided meditation workshops. A wellness brand wanted to host a monthly “digital retreat.” A creator asked to use the pavilion as the venue for a sound-healing event. Each partnership brought income. Each event brought new visitors. Her land value tripled within two months.

As Rina watched her sanctuary fill with glowing avatars floating peacefully above the water, she realized she had built a place of calm inside a chaotic digital universe—a place people cherished. A place that earned her more income in a week than her real job paid in a month.

One evening, Torin returned to visit. He stepped into the pavilion, looked around, and smiled warmly. "You've done well."

"I didn't think I could," Rina admitted. "I don't have experience in building or business."

Torin shook his head gently. "You had vision. That is the only real currency in this world."

Rina gazed out over the Moonlit River, watching reflections ripple beneath the lanterns she had placed. For the first time, she felt she had created something meaningful—not just code or pixels, but an experience that touched people. A digital sanctuary that brought peace to strangers around the world.

And as passive income continued to flow in, she realized something else: this wasn't just a parcel of land. It was the turning point of her life. A reminder that in the metaverse, anyone can build something beautiful. Anyone can earn. Anyone can transform a simple piece of virtual land into an empire—one glowing lantern at a time.

Chapter 4

Building, Renting, and Selling Virtual Businesses

One of the most powerful ways to earn income in the metaverse—both active and passive—is by building virtual businesses. Unlike digital land alone, which provides value primarily through renting or appreciation, virtual businesses generate revenue through ongoing commercial activity. These businesses can take many forms: virtual shops, clubs, training centers, studios, galleries, gaming arenas, service-based hubs, and entire automated experiences. The metaverse functions like a living economy where businesses operate 24/7, attracting global visitors across different time zones. Once built, virtual businesses can be rented out to other creators, operated for profit, or sold as complete turn-key digital assets. Understanding how to create, structure, and monetize these businesses is essential if you want to thrive in the virtual economy.

The first step is selecting your **business model**. There are three main types of virtual businesses: (1) businesses that sell digital goods, such as wearables, art, NFTs, templates, or in-world tools; (2) businesses that offer services or experiences, such as entertainment venues, educational spaces, retreat centers, or social hubs; and (3) businesses that generate traffic for monetization, such as advertising spaces, lounges, news boards, or tourist attractions. Each model serves a different purpose and caters to different audiences. To choose the right model, identify your strengths: Are you a creator who can design digital items? Are you an educator who can teach inside a virtual classroom? Are you an organizer who wants to host events? Or are you an investor looking to build a space and then let others run the operations?

After choosing your model, the next step is selecting **the platform** where your business will live. Decentraland, The Sandbox, Spatial, VRChat, Roblox, Horizon Worlds, Mona, and other platforms each offer unique economics. Decentraland is ideal for art galleries, fashion brands, and education-focused experiences. The Sandbox is strong for gaming, voxel-based builds, and branded partnerships. VRChat is excellent for immersive social experiences. Roblox offers scalability for younger audiences and developers. Spatial appeals to professional and creative communities. The platform you choose determines the tools you will use, the type of audience you will attract, and the monetization options available to you. Before building, spend time exploring each world to understand the visual culture, design styles, and popular locations. Next, you must focus on **design and development**. Virtual businesses thrive on two principles:

atmosphere and functionality. Atmosphere includes your lighting, textures, music, color palette, and overall visual appeal. Functionality includes user flow, interactivity, accessibility, and what actions visitors can take. A digital gallery must display art clearly and allow easy navigation. A virtual nightclub needs immersive lighting, music responsiveness, and dance areas. A training center must contain presentation screens, seating, and audio zones. A mini-game arena requires portals, leaderboards, and reward systems. Keep in mind that metaverse users have short attention spans; they decide within seconds whether they want to stay in your space. Your design must instantly communicate purpose, quality, and experience.

Once your business is built, you can choose between **operating it yourself**, **renting it**, or **selling it**. Operating the business yourself gives you full control over monetization, branding, customer relationships, and long-term income. For example, if you run a virtual store, you can update products whenever you want. If you host events, you can partner with sponsors and creators. If you run a gaming experience, you can create seasonal updates and keep players returning. Operating your own business allows for ongoing revenue but requires maintenance and active involvement.

Renting your virtual business is one of the most powerful forms of passive income. Many creators build high-quality structures—shops, clubs, venues, schools, and event spaces—that they never intend to operate personally. Instead, they rent them to influencers, DJs, artists, teachers, brands, or commercial partners who want a ready-to-use space without building their own. Rental contracts can be weekly, monthly, or tied to specific events. Because the owner does not handle operations, this income is nearly passive. Businesses located in high-traffic areas command premium rents, and themed or highly polished builds appeal to clients who want prestige and convenience.

Selling virtual businesses is another lucrative opportunity. Think of it like flipping real estate: you build a complete business—structures, interior design, branding, signage, and interactive features—and sell it as a package. Buyers often pay high premiums for turnkey businesses because it saves them time, design costs, and builder fees. A fully developed nightclub with lighting, music syncing, dance floors, VIP rooms, and a branded exterior can sell for significantly more than the value of the land beneath it. The same is true for art galleries, boutique fashion stores, gaming arenas, and wellness retreats. When building to sell, focus on uniqueness, polish, modular layouts, and ease of use.

Another powerful strategy is **business franchising**. In the metaverse, franchising is easier than in the real world because digital templates can be duplicated instantly. If you create a successful business model—such as a popular café, a meditation pod, a gaming experience, or a branded shop—you can sell licenses or NFT-based franchise rights. Buyers receive copies of your business template, brand assets, instructions, and permissions. You can charge upfront fees, ongoing royalties, or token-based membership access. Franchising allows your brand to expand across multiple parcels and platforms while generating passive recurring income.

Marketing your virtual business is crucial to long-term success. Use social media, Discord communities, in-world events, influencer collaborations, and wearable drops to promote your space. Participate in platform festivals, theme weeks, gallery nights, game tournaments, or brand activations. The metaverse rewards visibility. The more people visit your business, the higher your chances of generating sales, rentals, or sponsorships. A well-marketed business becomes a destination, not just a structure.

Finally, understand that virtual businesses scale infinitely. Unlike physical businesses, which require physical locations, staff, inventory, and overhead, virtual businesses can grow without limits. You can duplicate your builds, expand across multiple worlds, automate your processes, and sell unlimited digital goods. A single concept can turn into an empire. The metaverse eliminates traditional barriers—meaning anyone with creativity, strategy, and consistency can build a profitable business from scratch, even with no technical background. The next generation of digital entrepreneurs is already emerging inside virtual worlds. And with the right knowledge and vision, you can become one of them.

The Nightclub Made of Stars

Jace Ellison had always dreamed of owning a nightclub, but real life made it impossible. Rent was too high, equipment too costly, and staffing too complicated. But everything changed the night he wandered into a metaverse party hosted on a floating island suspended high above a digital ocean. The walls shimmered like constellations, the music pulsed through the air like electricity, and avatars danced beneath a ceiling made of swirling galaxies. Jace felt his breath catch. He had never seen anything like it.

After the event ended, he approached the host—a confident avatar named ARIA, dressed in a glowing suit that looked like liquid chrome. "How did you build this?" Jace asked, still overwhelmed by the experience.

ARIA smiled. "I didn't build it. I rented it." She gestured around. "The owner created it as a ready-to-use venue. I just booked it for the night."

Jace stared at her. "You're telling me someone earns money just by renting out this place?"

"Every night," ARIA replied. "This venue is booked weeks in advance. People love it."

A spark ignited in Jace's mind. If someone else could build a nightclub inside the metaverse and rent it out, why couldn't he? He didn't have design skills or experience, but the idea refused to leave him. He spent the next few weeks exploring worlds, studying popular venues, visiting clubs, lounges, and music stages. Some were flashy. Some were minimalistic. Some were packed. Some were empty. But he noticed one thing: experiences mattered more than complexity.

Jace bought a small parcel of virtual land in a platform known for its music events. It wasn't the largest, the fanciest, or the most central—but it had potential. Every night after work, he logged in and tinkered with free building tools. His first designs looked like broken boxes and mismatched neon displays. But he practiced. He experimented. He learned. Slowly, the shape of his dream began to form.

He built a circular dance floor that glowed with every beat of the song. He created floating holograms that burst into shapes when avatars walked through them. He crafted a bar made of drifting star fragments. He placed a DJ stage that hovered above the crowd like a meteor. When he finally finished, he stepped back and looked at his creation—a nightclub suspended in the sky, wrapped in constellations and lights. He named it *THE ASTRAL ROOM.*

With uncertainty in his chest, he posted a simple message in a community forum: *"New venue available for rent. Affordable rates. Stunning views."* He didn't expect much. Maybe one person would inquire. Maybe none.

The next morning, he woke to eighteen messages.

Artists wanted to host album launches. DJs wanted weekly residencies. A wedding planner wanted an otherworldly venue for a metaverse ceremony. Jace sat there, stunned. He wasn't prepared for this level of demand, but he adapted. He created a rental calendar. He established rules. He added customizable lighting options. Within days, *The Astral Room* was fully booked.

One night, Jace entered the club to check on an event. Avatars danced beneath the pulsing nebula lights. The DJ controlled the stars with every beat. Guests took selfies on the floating balcony overlooking a glowing planet below. For a moment, Jace stood quietly at the back, overwhelmed. He had built this. He had created a place where thousands of people gathered—not in the real world, but in a world that felt real in its own way.

As his rental income grew, Jace expanded. He built a second venue: a cyberpunk lounge carved into the side of a digital skyscraper. Then a beach club on a virtual island. Then a futuristic opera hall suspended in zero gravity. Each venue attracted its own audience. Each generated recurring profit. Each became a piece of Jace's growing digital empire.

Months later, ARIA visited *The Astral Room* again, this time as a guest. She found Jace standing near the entrance, watching the dancers below. "You've built something special," she told him.

Jace smiled. "I never thought I'd own a nightclub."

ARIA looked around at the swirling galaxies he had created. "You don't own just one," she said. "You own a universe of them."

Jace realized she was right. The metaverse had given him what the physical world never could: a chance to dream without limits, to build without boundaries, and to create a business that grew even while he slept. His nightclubs made of stars weren't just venues—they were proof that in the metaverse, imagination itself could become a business.

And as he stood there watching the lights flicker across happy avatars from around the world, he knew he had unlocked a future brighter than any nightclub could ever contain.

Chapter 5

Monetizing Virtual Events, Experiences, and Communities

Virtual events and experiences have become one of the most profitable income streams in the metaverse because they offer something no physical location can: global accessibility, infinite scalability, zero logistical limitations, and total creative freedom. The metaverse enables events that would cost millions in the real world—Massive concerts, multi-stage festivals, arena tournaments, immersive conferences, interactive workshops, and social gatherings—to be created at a fraction of the cost. More importantly, these events can be monetized endlessly through ticket sales, sponsorships, VIP upgrades, digital merchandise, partnerships, and post-event content sales. To profit from this opportunity, you must understand how virtual experiences are designed, marketed, structured, and monetized.

The first principle is understanding **why people attend metaverse events**. Unlike typical Zoom calls or livestreams, metaverse events offer immersion. Users attend not just to watch but to participate. They explore environments, interact with other avatars, complete challenges, unlock rewards, dance, socialize, or learn. Successful events are built around one of five core motivations: entertainment, education, networking, competition, or community bonding. The stronger your event addresses one or more of these motivations, the higher your attendance and revenue will be. Even simple events—a DJ night, a meet-up, a workshop—can attract hundreds if the experience feels meaningful, visually impressive, or socially exciting.

The second principle is crafting the **experience design**. Metaverse users crave environments that stimulate the senses and spark curiosity. When designing an event space, focus on atmosphere—lighting, music, storytelling, interactivity, and thematic consistency. A virtual concert may use holographic effects that pulse with the beat. A meditation retreat may float above a serene landscape. A fashion show might use futuristic runways with dynamic lighting and teleportation effects. Unlike real-world venues, your environment can defy gravity, physics, and architecture. Make your space unforgettable. Strong experience design improves visitor engagement, event reputation, and long-term revenue.

Next, you must understand **monetization structures**. There are several ways to earn money from virtual events. The simplest is **ticket sales**—charging an entry fee. This works well for concerts, classes, seminars, and private experiences. Another major revenue stream is **VIP upgrades**, offering special access, exclusive zones, backstage meetups, or bonus content. Sponsorships are one of the highest-paying streams; brands pay creators to host events because it gives them exposure, foot traffic, and credibility inside virtual worlds. You can also earn money from **in-event purchases**, such as wearable drops, merchandise NFTs, emotes, digital drinks, or themed accessories. If your event attracts a large audience, **advertising slots** on screens, posters, or holo-panels become valuable assets. Additionally, creators often charge **rental fees** to event hosts for using their virtual venue. Combining multiple monetization channels can turn even modest events into lucrative ones.

Another essential element is **community building**. The metaverse thrives on communities—groups centered around shared interests, music, art, education, gaming, culture, goals, or lifestyles. A strong community ensures repeat attendance, word-of-mouth referrals, and long-term loyalty. Successful creators build Discord servers, social hubs, membership NFTs, or ongoing meetups to cultivate their audience. Hosting regular events—weekly parties, monthly workshops, recurring tournaments—keeps a community active and engaged. A well-managed community also attracts sponsors seeking access to your audience. In the metaverse, community is currency. A community that trusts you will buy your products, attend your events, and support your expansions across multiple worlds.

Marketing is crucial. Even the best event will fail if no one knows about it. Promotion in the metaverse requires a multi-platform strategy. You must post announcements on Discord, Twitter, Instagram, YouTube, and the platform's native events calendar. Collaborate with influencers, DJs, artists, educators, or other community leaders who can bring their audiences. Use wearable airdrops—free digital items—to promote events; many creators release limited-edition badges or accessories that allow holders to claim perks during the event. Host pre-event meetups or open rehearsals to generate hype. The metaverse rewards visibility, so consistent and creative marketing is essential for success.

Another powerful monetization method is offering **event services**. Even if you don't want to host events yourself, you can earn money by providing event-building services. This includes stage design, lighting setup, audio integration, NPC scripting, experience design, and technical troubleshooting. Many creators offer packages that include venue rental, decoration, music, staffing, and custom branding. Because many event hosts lack technical skills, they are willing to pay creators who can bring their vision to life. Event creation services can become a steady income stream for talented builders. Post-event monetization is often overlooked but highly profitable. Events can be recorded and transformed into replay experiences, highlight videos, recap galleries, or collectible NFTs. You can sell digital posters, moments, backstage clips, or special emotes that memorialize the event. You can even turn popular events into ongoing series with paid subscriptions. The metaverse allows creators to repurpose content endlessly, turning a single event into multiple revenue streams.

Finally, understand that metaverse events are scalable. You can host events for 10 people or 10,000 people without worrying about venue capacity, physical logistics, weather, staffing, or travel restrictions. This scalability means your income potential is limited only by your imagination and marketing. Metaverse event hosts who master this model often expand into multiple worlds, run event agencies, build permanent venues, launch branded experiences, or create recurring festivals that become cultural landmarks in virtual space.

Mastering virtual events and experiences is one of the most powerful financial opportunities in the metaverse. It combines creativity, social energy, and entrepreneurship. If you can make people feel something—excitement, wonder, connection, joy, escape—you can build a profitable metaverse business that thrives endlessly.

The Festival of a Thousand Lights

Luna Ramirez had never planned to host a festival. She logged into the metaverse just to explore, curious about the glowing cities and floating landscapes she had heard so much about. One night, she wandered into a small gathering of avatars dancing around floating lanterns beside a shimmering lake. The music was soft, the lights gentle, the atmosphere peaceful. Luna sat down beside the water, feeling a sense of comfort she hadn't felt in months. It reminded her of the lantern festivals her grandmother used to take her to as a child.

As she watched the lanterns drift upward, she whispered to herself, "What if there was a festival like this... but bigger?" She imagined a sky full of lights, thousands of avatars celebrating together, the entire world glowing like a universe on fire. The idea was only a daydream—until an avatar sitting nearby turned and said, "That would be beautiful." His name was Kai. He smiled. "If you build it, I'll help you."

Luna had no experience creating anything digital. She wasn't a designer, an event planner, or a builder. But she had a vision—a world filled with light, music, and connection. She and Kai began meeting each night, exploring empty parcels of land, looking for the right spot. Finally, they found it: a floating island suspended over a galaxy-like abyss, with star clusters swirling below. Luna felt her heart race. "This is it," she whispered.

She spent weeks learning to build: platforms, lanterns, waterfalls of light, floating walkways, color-changing skies. Kai scripted interactive lantern releases, where attendees could send their own glowing light up into the sky. Luna designed areas for meditation, dancing, music, and storytelling. Every night, she added something new—a spiral staircase of stars, a bridge of glass, a garden of glowing flowers. The island slowly transformed into a dreamscape.

Finally, she announced her event: **THE FESTIVAL OF A THOUSAND LIGHTS — A Night of Wonder and Togetherness.** She didn't expect much. Maybe a few curious avatars would show up.

The night of the festival arrived. Luna logged in early, nervous. The island glowed softly beneath her feet, the lights pulsing gently. Then she heard footsteps. One avatar arrived. Then three. Then ten. Then fifty. Luna's heart pounded. Within minutes, hundreds of avatars filled the island. Lanterns floated upward like fireflies. Musicians played live sets. Strangers laughed, meditated, danced, hugged, and explored the dreamlike world she had created.

Then the impossible happened.

The platform administrators messaged her: "Your event has gone viral. Expect heavy traffic." Within an hour, thousands of avatars flooded the island. Luna stood frozen, tears in her eyes. She couldn't believe it. The entire sky above her filled with lanterns—so many that the virtual night shimmered like a living constellation.

Attendees began messaging her nonstop: "Can I donate?" "Will you host another?" "Can we sponsor this event?" "Do you rent this venue?" "Would you host our brand activation here?" Luna realized she had accidentally built a business.

In the weeks that followed, she was approached by wellness companies, musicians, educators, and even a virtual travel agency that wanted to partner on monthly events. She rented the island for private celebrations. She sold collectible lantern NFTs from the festival. She launched membership passes for early access to future events. Revenue flowed in faster than she ever imagined.

One evening, Kai joined her on the floating bridge overlooking the galaxy beneath them. Lanterns from the last event drifted slowly upward, shimmering. “You created something magical,” he said.

Luna smiled softly. “I just wanted to make something beautiful.”

“And look what it became,” Kai replied. She gazed out over the glowing sky, realizing that her childhood memories had blossomed into a living world—a business built from dreams and light. She hadn’t just created an event. She had built a community. A sanctuary. A phenomenon.

The Festival of a Thousand Lights became a monthly tradition, with visitors from around the world attending each one. Luna’s island grew, her income grew, and her purpose grew. What started as a whisper beside a lake had become a beacon in the metaverse.

And as another thousand lanterns floated into the digital sky, Luna knew she had found her calling—creating experiences that brought light to others, and in doing so, illuminating her own path.

Chapter 6

Creating, Selling, and Licensing Digital Goods

Digital goods are the backbone of the metaverse economy, functioning as the primary assets people buy, sell, wear, collect, and use. Unlike physical goods, digital goods have no manufacturing costs, no shipping fees, no inventory limits, and no physical constraints. A single digital item can be sold thousands of times, across multiple platforms, with automated delivery and payment processing. This makes digital goods one of the most scalable, profitable, and beginner-friendly income streams in the metaverse. To succeed in this category, you must understand the types of digital goods, how they gain value, how to create them, and how to market and monetize them effectively.

The first category is **wearables and avatar fashion**, which includes clothing, accessories, hairstyles, skins, effects, emotes, and cosmetic items. These items hold value because they allow users to express identity and status. Limited-edition wearables often appreciate in value, especially when created by established designers or tied to major events. To succeed in wearable creation, you must pay attention to trends, visual culture, and platform-specific design requirements. Each metaverse has unique technical specifications, file formats, and polygon limits. However, most platforms support intuitive drag-and-drop or template-based creation tools, making wearable design accessible to beginners.

The second category is **structures and templates**, which include houses, offices, stores, clubs, galleries, stages, gardens, and modular building assets. Many users want to own virtual spaces without building them from scratch, creating strong demand for ready-made templates. A well-designed building with appealing aesthetics can sell repeatedly. Templates are especially profitable because they require no technical updates once created, aside from optional expansions. Builders often create themed collections—such as cyberpunk apartments, futuristic lounges, nature sanctuaries, or minimalist studios—to reach niche audiences.

The third category is **NFT collectibles**, which include art, characters, tools, badges, utilities, membership passes, and limited-edition items. Collectibles gain value through scarcity, community demand, storytelling, and cultural relevance. NFT creators must think beyond the artwork; they must build lore, meaning, or utility behind each token. Collectors care about uniqueness, rarity tiers, aesthetics, and what the NFT unlocks—access, perks, identity roles, or community benefits. NFTs can generate recurring income through secondary-sale royalties, making them one of the most powerful long-term digital good strategies.

Another lucrative category is **audio assets**, including soundtracks, loops, ambient environments, sound effects, and music packs. Virtual worlds need audio for immersion. Event hosts, builders, game creators, and experience designers rely on purchasable audio to complete their spaces. Creating audio assets requires no coding and minimal equipment. A simple ambient loop created once can generate income for years through licensing. Musicians often create thematic packs—for example, lo-fi beats for cafes, space ambience for sci-fi worlds, or peaceful soundscapes for meditation hubs.

The fifth category is **game assets**, which include weapons, tools, creatures, furniture, props, animations, terrain packs, or interactable objects used inside mini-games or virtual experiences. Many creators prefer buying premade assets instead of modeling everything from scratch. Selling game assets requires attention to detail and understanding platform compatibility, but the scalability is massive. A single sci-fi prop pack can be used across dozens of worlds. Game asset creators often develop large libraries they sell on marketplaces like Roblox, Unity, Unreal-based metaverses, and decentralized ecosystems. Another major category is **scripts and interactive systems**, such as portals, teleporters, NPCs, scoreboards, mini-game frameworks, shop systems, or environmental effects. These digital tools allow creators to enhance their spaces without coding from scratch. Scripting assets tend to sell at higher price points due to their functionality. Creators who understand simple coding or use AI-assisted development can build powerful interactive tools to sell repeatedly.

To profit from digital goods, you must master **value creation**. Value comes from quality, scarcity, relevance, branding, and social proof. Quality means your design is visually polished, optimized, and bug-free. Scarcity increases desirability and resale value. Relevance means your item fits current trends or solves a need. Branding helps users recognize your style and trust your work. Social proof comes from community engagement, influencer collaborations, and event integrations.

Marketing digital goods is just as important as creating them. Great creators promote their items through social media, Discord channels, in-world events, wearable drops, influencer partnerships, and themed releases. Themed collections—holiday packs, futuristic lines, seasonal drops—drive stronger engagement. Collaborations with DJs, artists, game creators, or brands give your goods additional exposure. You can also host pop-up shops or launch parties in your virtual spaces to showcase your items in immersive ways.

One of the most powerful strategies is **licensing**. Instead of selling digital goods outright, you can license them to creators, venues, or businesses. Licensing allows others to use your assets while you retain ownership. This is common for audio packs, environmental assets, characters, animations, and scripts. Licensing generates recurring income without sacrificing intellectual property. Creating bundles—such as "Creator Starter Packs" or "Event Essentials Packs"—can attract buyers who want multiple assets at once.

Selling digital goods is scalable across multiple worlds. A wearable made for one platform can be adapted for others. A building template can be sold in Decentraland, Spatial, and Horizon Worlds with minor adjustments. Audio packs can be used anywhere. The more platforms you cover, the more revenue streams you create. Eventually, successful creators build full brands, complete with storefronts, websites, social communities, and collections spanning different metaverse ecosystems.

The metaverse rewards creators who understand aesthetics, user behavior, and digital culture. You don't need advanced skills to start—just curiosity, creativity, and consistency. Once you release your first digital item, you enter a world where every asset you create can become part of a growing digital empire. Digital goods are the future of online commerce—and those who understand how to create and monetize them are positioned to control one of the most lucrative opportunities of the next decade.

The Artisan of Infinite Things

Sora Liang loved to create things. As a child, she painted on scraps of paper, sculpted tiny clay figures, and stitched miniature outfits for her toys. But life pushed her toward practicality. She worked in accounting, kept her head down, and rarely found time for creativity. Yet the quiet ache for making beautiful things never left her. One rainy evening, feeling restless, Sora logged into a metaverse platform for the first time, expecting nothing more than mild distraction.

She appeared inside a bustling digital marketplace—glowing stalls, floating signs, neon-lit walkways, and avatars browsing treasures that shimmered in ways no physical object could. She wandered from booth to booth, fascinated by the creativity around her. A dazzling jacket that sparkled like meteor dust. A tiny dragon creature that followed its owner. A meditation space shaped like a lotus made of light. She felt a familiar spark ignite inside her, something she hadn't felt in years.

At one booth, she noticed an elegant pair of glowing butterfly wings. She gasped. "Did you make these?" she asked the booth owner, an avatar with shimmering silver hair named ILYRA. Ilyra nodded proudly. "Yep. Took me two hours. Sold over six hundred already."

Sora blinked. "Six hundred? Of the same pair?"

"Digital goods," Ilyra said with a grin. "Make it once. Sell it forever."

The idea hit Sora like lightning. A world where creativity wasn't limited by cost, materials, or inventory. A world where imagination could be multiplied infinitely. A world she had unknowingly been searching for her entire life.

Sora began learning obsessively. She watched tutorials, joined creator Discords, asked questions in forums, and practiced late into the night. Her first creation was a simple glowing bracelet. It wasn't perfect—the edges were uneven and the lighting was too bright. But she felt proud. She uploaded it, set a modest price, and logged off.

The next morning, she woke to five notifications. She had made sales. Real income from something she had designed. For the first time in years, she felt alive.

Her confidence grew. She created earrings shaped like tiny galaxies, rings that glowed with shifting colors, hairpieces made of floating light petals, and dresses with animated patterns inspired by constellations. She curated her items into themed collections—Celestial, Blossom, Spirit, Dawn. Each drop attracted more buyers. Soon, influencers started wearing her designs to events. Screenshots of her outfits circulated online. Her store became known as **SORA'S SANCTUM**.

But Sora wanted more than fashion. She wanted to build entire worlds. She designed a serene virtual tea garden nestled among cherry-blossom trees made of pixels and wind. She created a meditation dome filled with drifting fireflies of light. She crafted modular furniture sets for creators building their own spaces. Everything she crafted held a piece of her heart.

One day, a popular event organizer messaged her. "Your audio tracks from the Blossom Garden... can we license them for our monthly retreat?" Sora blinked. "My audio tracks?" She had composed simple ambient loops for her spaces—soft wind chimes, trickling water, calming tones. She never imagined someone would pay to use them.

She agreed, and soon other creators began licensing her assets too—sound packs, foliage assets, lantern models, animated props. She realized she was no longer just selling individual items. She was licensing creations across the metaverse.

Months passed. Sora's Sanctum expanded into a multi-world brand. She opened a flagship store in a glowing floating city. She collaborated with other artists, musicians, and builders. A digital museum even hosted an exhibition of her items titled *The Beauty of Light.* Sora walked through the gallery in awe, seeing dozens of her creations displayed like art pieces—each one a reminder that she had found her calling.

One evening, she returned to the empty marketplace where her journey had begun. The same stall where she first saw the butterfly wings now stood empty. She closed her eyes and whispered, "Thank you," to the world that had given her back her creativity.

As she looked around the glowing city, filled with avatars wearing her designs, living in spaces she built, and listening to music she composed, she realized she had become something she never expected: **the artisan of infinite things**. In the metaverse, her creativity had no limits. Her income had no ceiling. Her possibilities had no end.

And Sora knew she would spend the rest of her life crafting worlds of beauty, one digital creation at a time.

Chapter 7

Building Your Personal Brand and Marketing Your Metaverse Income Streams

The metaverse is a rapidly expanding universe filled with creators, entrepreneurs, artists, developers, educators, entertainers, and investors. With so many people entering the space, one of the most important steps to achieving long-term success is building a strong personal brand. A personal brand is more than a username or a logo—it is your identity in the digital world. It tells people who you are, what you create, and why they should trust you. Building a brand allows you to stand out, gain recognition, build community, and attract opportunities such as collaborations, sponsorships, buyers, and clients. In the metaverse, branding is not optional—it is essential.

The first foundation of personal branding is **clarity**. You must know who you are within the metaverse economy. Are you a builder? A wearable designer? A photographer? A DJ? A storyteller? A collector? A land developer? A community organizer? A teacher? Or a mix of several roles? Clarity allows people to associate your name with a skill, experience, or value. Without clarity, your audience will be confused about what you offer. You don't have to limit yourself to one niche forever, but choosing a primary area of focus helps you grow faster. Successful metaverse creators often create simple brand identities: "The Cyberpunk Wearable Designer," "The Virtual Architect," "The Galaxy DJ," or "The Zen Builder." When your audience can describe you in a sentence, your brand becomes easier to remember and recommend.

The second pillar is **identity design**, which includes your avatar style, your brand colors, your logo, your nickname, and the overall visual aesthetic of your work. In the metaverse, your avatar is a walking business card. It should reflect your style, your creativity, and your message. If you design elegant wearable fashion, your avatar should look fashion-forward. If you build meditation worlds, your avatar should evoke calmness. If you run futuristic nightclubs, your avatar should reflect that world. Consistency helps people recognize you instantly across events, platforms, and social channels. You should also maintain consistent branding in your profile photos, your banners, your store thumbnails, and your marketing posts.

The next step is establishing **social presence**. Your brand must exist beyond the metaverse. Successful creators grow through platforms like Discord, X (Twitter), Instagram,

TikTok, YouTube, Twitch, and platform-specific forums. Each platform serves a purpose. Discord builds community and allows for private communication. X and Instagram are great for announcements and quick updates. TikTok and YouTube are ideal for tutorials, behind-the-scenes building sessions, time-lapses, or promotional videos. A strong social presence increases visibility, attracts followers, and drives traffic to your events, stores, and experiences. Consistency is key—post updates, work-in-progress images, short teasers, and community polls often.

Another central component of personal branding is **community building**. Communities are the lifeblood of the metaverse. Whether you have 50 followers or 50,000, your community will support your launches, attend your events, buy your items, and share your work. Build your community with intention. Engage with your supporters. Respond to messages. Host small meetups. Give early access to your drops. Reward loyal fans. People don't follow brands—they follow emotion, connection, and authenticity. The stronger your community, the faster your income grows.

To market your income streams effectively, you must master the art of **storytelling**. Every successful brand has a narrative. When you release a wearable item, tell the story behind it. When you launch a virtual world, explain your inspiration. When you build a gallery, share how you designed it. Humans connect to stories—emotion sells. In the metaverse, storytelling is even more powerful because it ties into immersion. Your brand story becomes part of the worlds you build and the items you create. Share your journey. Share your mistakes. Share your wins. People love to watch creators grow, and your story becomes a magnet for supporters.

Collaboration is another essential branding tool. The metaverse thrives on partnerships. Team up with DJs, artists, fashion designers, builders, and influencers to launch co-branded products or host joint events. Collaborations expand your audience and create opportunities you cannot achieve alone. A simple collaboration can double your reach instantly. Cross-promotion helps both creators grow. Choose partners whose values and aesthetics complement yours for the strongest impact.

Marketing your work involves **launch strategy**. Every release should feel like an event. Tease upcoming drops with previews, countdowns, beta access, or behind-the-scenes footage. Host launch parties inside your virtual spaces. Offer early-bird pricing for your community. Give influencers promo versions to showcase. Build anticipation. The stronger the hype, the higher the sales. Many creators decorate their spaces with giant holograms or billboards advertising their new products.

This makes every visitor feel like they've walked into a launch event.

In addition, visibility inside the metaverse is essential. Attend major events. Participate in seasonal festivals. Explore worlds where your audience hangs out. Talk to other creators. Join building competitions. Leave positive feedback in other people's galleries. Become part of your world's culture. The more avatars that recognize your name, the faster your brand grows.

A crucial part of branding is **trust-building**. Honor your commitments. Deliver quality. Be transparent with customers. Handle disputes professionally. Avoid overpromising. Ask for feedback and improve. The metaverse rewards creators with good reputations—and punishes those who betray trust. The more trust you build, the more your income streams multiply. Brands, sponsors, investors, and high-profile creators will want to work with you when they see you as reliable and consistent.

Finally, long-term branding comes from **scaling your identity across multiple worlds**. Don't limit yourself to one platform. Build worlds in different metaverses. Sell items in cross-world marketplaces. Expand your brand identity into new ecosystems. Become known as a multi-world creator. This multiplies your reach and cements your reputation as a metaverse authority. The creators who dominate the future are those who spread their presence across every major virtual world. Building a personal brand is your greatest asset in the metaverse. It amplifies every income stream—land development, wearables, events, digital goods, and collaborations. A strong brand opens doors to opportunities you didn't know existed. When people recognize your name, trust your quality, and love your story, your metaverse empire grows effortlessly. Branding is not just part of the metaverse economy—it is the engine that powers your success.

The Avatar in the Golden Jacket

Niko Reyes had always been quiet. In the physical world, he kept to himself, blending into crowds, never calling attention to his presence. But in the metaverse, everything changed the moment he put on the golden jacket.

He didn't buy it for status or attention. He bought it because it reminded him of his grandmother's favorite saying: *"Wear your light, even if the world doesn't see it yet."* The jacket shimmered like liquid gold, reflecting the light in hypnotic patterns. When Niko wore it, he felt bold—alive in a way he never felt outside the virtual world.

One night, Niko attended a digital music festival inside a floating arena shaped like a lotus made of light. Avatars danced through beams of color, holograms burst into shapes, and music pulsed through the sky. When Niko arrived, something unexpected happened: dozens of avatars turned to look at him.

"Whoa—where did you get that jacket?" "That's incredible!" "Are you a designer?"

Niko blushed behind his headset. "No... I'm nobody. Just someone exploring."

A DJ named ARX approached him. "That jacket has presence," he said. "You should make it your signature." "My signature?" Niko asked. "Your brand."

The idea lingered in Niko's mind. Could he build a brand around something as simple as a jacket? He wasn't a designer. He didn't host events. He wasn't famous. But the metaverse didn't care about the past—only the creativity you brought into its worlds.

The next day, Niko created a small profile page and named himself **GOLDEN_NIKO**. He took pictures of his avatar in different worlds—the neon city, the snowy mountains, the crystal desert. He wrote a simple bio: *"I explore worlds and* *share the light I find."* He posted his first introduction on Discord communities and Twitter. He expected nothing.

Instead, people followed him.

They liked his photos. They commented on his jacket. They asked for world recommendations. They invited him to events. Niko was stunned. For the first time, he felt seen—not just as a person, but as a presence.

Encouraged, he started exploring worlds daily and documenting them. He reviewed galleries. He showcased creators. He offered positivity and encouragement. Slowly, he became known not as a builder or designer, but as a **guide**—someone who found beauty and highlighted it.

But something else began happening.

Creators began messaging him: "Would you wear my jacket in your next post?" "Can we collaborate?" "We'd love to sponsor your next world tour."

People trusted him because he was authentic. He didn't promote things he didn't believe in. He praised creators genuinely. He shared stories of what inspired him. His brand became a beacon of positivity in the metaverse.

Eventually, he launched the **Golden Light Community**—a group dedicated to exploring new worlds, uplifting creators, and celebrating virtual artistry. Within months, thousands joined. They hosted meetups, photography tours, fashion nights, and meditation gatherings. Brands approached Niko for collaborations. DJs invited him to appear at their events. Wearable designers paid him to showcase their items. World builders asked him to host launch parties in their spaces.

One evening, after a major event where he had been welcomed like a celebrity, Niko walked alone to the edge of a digital cliff overlooking a shimmering neon sea. He removed his golden jacket and held it in his digital hands. The light danced across its fabric.

Kai, one of the earliest members of his community, appeared beside him. "You've come a long way," Kai said. Niko shook his head softly. "I still feel like that quiet guy who didn't know where he belonged." Kai smiled. "And look what happened when you let your light show."

Niko looked out at the glowing horizon. His brand, his community, his influence—all of it had grown from a single spark: wearing something that made him feel alive. The jacket wasn't the source of his success. It was the belief he gained from it. The metaverse hadn't changed him—it had allowed him to become who he truly was.

As he put the golden jacket back on, the world around him reflected the glow. And Niko knew, deep down, that he had become exactly what his grandmother once told him to be:

A light the world could finally see.

Chapter 8

Investing in Metaverse Tokens, DAOs, and Emerging Economies

Investing in the metaverse goes beyond simply buying land or selling digital items. A major portion of the metaverse economy is driven by **tokens**, **decentralized autonomous organizations (DAOs)**, and **emerging digital economies** that operate like miniature nations within virtual worlds. Understanding how to invest strategically in these systems is essential for long-term wealth building. While it may feel complex at first, the fundamentals are much simpler than they appear. The metaverse runs on digital currencies, governance tokens, staking pools, decentralized voting systems, asset-backed NFTs, and new economic models that allow ordinary users to become investors and co-owners of ecosystems rather than passive participants.

The foundation of metaverse investing lies in **platform tokens**. These are cryptocurrencies used within specific virtual worlds. For example, MANA is used in Decentraland, SAND in The Sandbox, ROBUX in Roblox's marketplace, and other decentralized worlds use their own native tokens. These tokens have utility—they are used to purchase land, pay for wearable minting, join events, buy digital goods, stake assets, or participate in governance. The value of a platform token is tied to the growth, activity, and adoption of the world it belongs to. When more people build, play, or transact inside a metaverse, token value tends to increase. Investing early in promising worlds can lead to significant long-term returns, but token volatility requires careful research and risk management.

Another major opportunity is **staking**, which allows investors to lock tokens or digital assets for passive yield. Many metaverse economies reward stakers with additional tokens, voting power, discounted marketplace fees, or exclusive access to features. Staking is like earning interest in a digital bank, except returns are often significantly higher. Some worlds allow staking land parcels or utility NFTs to earn rewards. Other platforms allow liquidity pool staking, providing stability to token markets in exchange for yield. While staking can generate predictable passive income, it requires understanding tokenomics, lock-up periods, and reward rates. Always research the ecosystem's credibility and security before staking.

One of the most revolutionary aspects of Web3 investing is **DAOs**—decentralized organizations run by token holders rather than CEOs or companies. DAOs allow users to collectively vote on decisions such as world development, funding proposals, event organization, ecosystem upgrades, or community initiatives. When you hold governance tokens, you essentially become a shareholder who can influence the direction of a virtual world. Many DAOs also distribute revenue to token holders—profits from land sales, partnerships, royalties, events, or treasury investments. Some DAOs even co-own massive digital assets like districts, game studios, or branded experiences. Investing in the right DAO gives you exposure to multiple income streams without needing to build anything yourself.

Another high-potential investment area is **emerging digital economies**, especially those tied to early-stage metaverse worlds, play-to-earn games, virtual job markets, decentralized freelance hubs, and creator-driven marketplaces. Early adopters often receive rewards for participating—such as airdrops, early access tokens, or discounted land sales. Some users become "founding citizens" of a virtual nation, unlocking long-term economic benefits. These early-phase opportunities can be extremely profitable, but they carry higher risk. Success requires reading whitepapers, analyzing roadmaps, evaluating teams, and understanding long-term vision.

You must also understand **asset-backed NFTs**, which are NFTs tied to real utility rather than just art. These include access passes, land deeds, yield-generating assets, or NFTs that unlock specific privileges in a virtual world. Asset-backed NFTs behave like digital property—owners can sell them, rent them, or stake them for returns. For example, an NFT may grant lifetime entry to a popular game, membership in a metaverse club, or ownership of an AI-driven NPC that works autonomously. These NFTs often become valuable long-term assets as demand increases.

Another strategy is **diversification**, which means spreading your investments across multiple metaverse worlds. Investing everything into one token or one world can be risky. Instead, build a portfolio of digital land, utility NFTs, platform tokens, DAO stakes, and yield-generating assets. Diversifying protects you from market downturns in any single ecosystem and increases your exposure to potential growth across multiple worlds.

Long-term success in metaverse investing requires evaluating **ecosystem fundamentals**, such as user activity, developer involvement, updates, partnerships, branding strength, marketplace volume, and community governance. High-quality worlds grow consistently. Weak worlds stagnate or collapse. Always invest based on real utility, not hype. Look for worlds that solve problems, empower creators, offer robust building tools, host active communities, and encourage economic activity.

Finally, remember that investing in the metaverse is both financial and emotional. You are not just buying assets—you are buying pieces of emerging civilizations. You are participating in decentralized cultures that will shape the future of online life. The creators, players, artists, teachers, builders, investors, and explorers of today are the pioneers of tomorrow. Investing wisely can turn you into a co-owner of the next great digital economies. And in the metaverse, early movers are often the ones who reap the greatest rewards.

The Treasury of Dawnfall City

Elias Draven had always been captivated by the idea of new worlds. Even as a child, he imagined cities built in the sky, kingdoms made of light, and marketplaces where traders dealt in stars instead of coins. So when he discovered the metaverse, he felt like he had finally stepped into the stories he dreamed of. But nothing captured his imagination more than the rumors of **Dawnfall City**, an emerging world still under development—an uncharted economy that only a few explorers knew about.

What intrigued Elias most wasn't the scenery or the architecture—it was the whisper that early citizens of Dawnfall City were becoming part-owners of the world itself. A friend sent him an invite to the city's private test environment. The moment Elias entered, he saw the potential. Towering cliffs glowed with amber light. Sky-lifts carried travelers between floating islands. Energy fields pulsed beneath the streets. The world felt incomplete, yet filled with promise.

As he walked through the city center, a golden emblem appeared in front of him: **THE DAWNFALL TREASURY – ENTRANCE FOR TOKEN HOLDERS ONLY.** Elias had no idea what it meant, but curiosity pulled him inside.

Inside the hall, a council of avatars gathered around a floating orb representing Dawnfall City's future. A voice echoed: "This treasury belongs to every citizen who believes in our world. Those who hold our governance tokens will shape its destiny." Elias watched as members voted on city expansions, new marketplaces, upgrades to the transportation system, and land distribution. Every vote shaped the world in real time.

A figure approached him—an avatar dressed in white crystalline armor. "You're new," she said. "I'm Lyra." "What is all this?" Elias asked. She smiled. "This is our DAO. Our decentralized government. If you join, you become a co-owner of Dawnfall City."

Elias felt his heart race. "Co-owner?"

Lyra nodded. "Yes. We vote on everything. And token holders earn from the city's entire economy—land sales, tourism fees, events, partnerships, staking rewards." She leaned closer. "We're building a world from scratch. And everyone who believes early will benefit later."

He spent days studying the whitepaper, analyzing the team, exploring the roadmap, and talking to early members. The more he learned, the more he believed this new world could flourish. Elias bought his first governance tokens—not many, but enough to become a citizen.

What happened next changed his life.

As Dawnfall City opened its gates to the public, users flooded in. Land sales exploded. Builders created shops, portals, galleries, sky gardens, and floating villas. A major gaming studio partnered to build a massive arena. A music artist announced a residency in the upper islands. The city grew every day—and with it, the token value.

Elias became deeply involved. He joined the treasury council, proposed new world features, helped approve sponsorships, and worked with other citizens to improve the economy. His tokens began generating passive rewards from events, land auctions, and marketplace fees.

One day, Lyra messaged him. "Come to the Grand Assembly Hall." When he arrived, the council gathered to unveil something extraordinary—a massive golden structure rising above the city. "This," Lyra said, "is the Dawnfall Infinite Vault. Our world's first automated revenue engine. It distributes earnings to all citizens."

Elias felt overwhelmed. He had become part of something greater—a world, a community, an economy, an emerging civilization. He wasn't just an investor. He was a builder of a digital nation.

Months passed. Dawnfall City transformed into one of the fastest-growing metaverse worlds. Elias's modest investment grew into a fortune. But the money mattered less than the meaning. He had helped create something real—something that would outlive him in digital form.

One evening, as Elias stood atop a floating balcony overlooking the illuminated city, Lyra appeared beside him. "You did well," she said softly. "I'm just one voice," Elias replied. Lyra shook her head. "One voice shapes a vote. A vote shapes a decision. A decision shapes a world."

Below them, Dawnfall City pulsed with life, glowing like a sunrise across an endless sky. Elias realized he had become something his childhood self would have never believed possible:

A founding citizen of a digital civilization—an investor in tomorrow.

Chapter 9

Freelancing, Remote Work, and Web3 Jobs in the Metaverse

As the metaverse evolves into a fully functioning digital economy, one of the fastest-growing opportunities is the rise of **Web3 jobs**, remote digital careers, and freelancing roles that exist entirely inside virtual worlds. Unlike traditional jobs, metaverse work is borderless, flexible, global, and available to anyone with skill, talent, or willingness to learn. Companies, creators, brands, DAOs, platforms, and individuals need specialized roles that support virtual development, world-building, content creation, marketing, education, community management, and technical support. These roles did not exist a decade ago, and new ones emerge constantly. Mastering the world of metaverse freelancing gives you access to a goldmine of high-paying opportunities—often with much lower competition than traditional online jobs.

The first step in understanding metaverse careers is recognizing the **categories of work**. The most common Web3 job roles include virtual world builders, 3D modelers, wearable designers, avatar stylists, sound designers, event coordinators, scripters, environment creators, game designers, and UX designers for immersive experiences. Beyond creative work, there are strategic and operational roles: blockchain analysts, community managers, DAO administrators, marketing specialists, partnership coordinators, Web3 social media managers, and brand ambassadors. There are also technical roles such as Solidity developers, smart contract auditors, and front-end or back-end developers for Web3 platforms. Whether you're artistic, technical, or business-oriented, there is a Web3 job category that fits your talents.

Next, you must understand **how hiring works in the metaverse**. Traditional resumes are less important. Your portfolio, your reputation, your contributions, and your presence inside virtual communities matter more. Many creators land jobs simply by showing up, helping others, participating in events, and sharing their builds or designs publicly. Most hiring comes from Discord communities, DAO forums, Twitter (X), and in-world social interactions. Employers want people who understand the culture of the platform, who can navigate virtual spaces confidently, and who demonstrate passion and creativity. Because Web3 is still young, many clients prefer someone enthusiastic and reliable over someone with a long formal resume.

A major advantage of metaverse freelancing is **income flexibility**. You can earn through hourly contracts, fixed-price projects, royalties, revenue share agreements, token compensation, NFT-based payments, performance bonuses, and partnership equity. Many metaverse freelancers earn in both crypto and fiat currency, giving them long-term upside in addition to immediate income. You can also stack revenue streams—design wearables for one client, build a world for another, manage events for a third, and earn royalties on digital goods at the same time.

One of the most in-demand roles today is **virtual world building**. Companies need environments for product launches, conferences, retail stores, entertainment venues, and community hubs. Builders are paid to design these spaces using platform-specific tools. You don't need to be a master 3D artist; many platforms use drag-and-drop or voxel-based creation tools. What matters is design sense, layout, atmosphere, and functionality. Builders often charge several hundred to several thousand dollars per build—sometimes more for premium worlds.

Wearable and avatar designers are also highly sought after. Brands, influencers, and creators want custom avatars, clothing, and accessories. These items become digital identity markers in the metaverse. A single wearable design can generate recurring royalties if sold in marketplaces. The demand for digital fashion will grow exponentially as more users enter virtual spaces, making it a powerful long-term career path.

Another fast-growing job category is **community management**, which involves moderating online communities, organizing events, answering questions, managing Discord servers, building fanbases, and creating engagement strategies. DAOs, NFT projects, metaverse platforms, and Web3 startups all need community managers. This role is ideal for people with strong communication, patience, and leadership skills. Many community managers earn stable salaries and bonuses.

Event professionals—DJs, hosts, public speakers, teachers, entertainers, and experience designers—can also earn impressive income. Virtual events need staff to plan, coordinate, manage stages, troubleshoot technical issues, and promote the event. Some earn tokens, others earn tips, and many secure sponsorship fees for hosting branded events. As metaverse festivals grow, event staff will become an essential and lucrative workforce.

A highly profitable and often overlooked category is **DAO governance and participation**. DAOs pay contributors to write proposals, analyze ecosystems, design governance systems, help manage treasuries, and perform operational roles. Many DAOs operate like decentralized companies, paying members for part-time or full-time work. These roles can include project management, analytics, event planning, treasury advisory, grant allocation, and marketing. Because DAOs value passion, new contributors can often start earning simply by being active and helpful.

To succeed as a freelancer, you must build a strong **portfolio**, even if you're a beginner. Use free tools to create sample worlds, wearables, designs, music tracks, or scripts. Create mock client projects. Display your portfolio in a virtual gallery, website, or social channel. Your portfolio will speak louder than any credentials.

Marketing yourself requires visibility. Join platform discords. Attend events. Introduce yourself in metaverse community hubs. Share your work regularly. Offer free samples or low-cost starter services to gain traction. As your reputation grows, raise your prices. Word-of-mouth spreads fast in tight-knit Web3 communities. If you deliver quality and professionalism, clients will refer you repeatedly.

The metaverse job market is still in its early stages. As virtual worlds expand, remote work opportunities will multiply. Soon, the metaverse will host virtual offices, corporate campuses, job fairs, and marketplaces for freelance talent. Those who establish themselves early will become leaders, earning premium rates and securing major partnerships.

The beauty of metaverse freelancing is that anyone can start—no degree, no location, no permission needed. If you bring value, skill, creativity, or reliability, the metaverse economy will reward you. This chapter is not just about making money—it is about shaping your digital career. The metaverse is a blank canvas, and the professionals who seize its opportunities today will become the pioneers of a new era of work.

The Girl Who Rebuilt the Sky District

Talia Kim had always been good with computers, but she never considered herself special. She worked long hours at a job she didn't love, answering emails and entering data while dreaming about something more. Every night, she logged into her favorite metaverse world—Sky District—a floating city resting on clouds made of shimmering light. It was the only place where she felt free.

One evening, she teleported into Sky District and gasped. Half the buildings were dark. Bridges flickered. Shops were closed. A message hovered in the air: **"SYSTEM UPDATE FAILURE — MAJOR REPAIRS NEEDED."**

"Looks abandoned," a voice said behind her.

Talia turned to see a tall avatar in emerald robes. His nametag read: **ORIN**.

"What happened?" she asked.

"A faulty update broke half the zone," Orin replied. "Most builders abandoned the project. The district is barely functional now."

Talia felt a strange sadness. Sky District had been her escape, her sanctuary. She couldn't stand the thought of it fading away.

"Can't someone fix it?" she asked.

Orin smiled faintly. "Someone could. But it would require rebuilding dozens of structures, optimizing scripts, and restoring assets. Most freelancers charge more than the district can afford."

Talia hesitated, then surprised herself with her next words. "I can do it."

Orin raised an eyebrow. "You?"

"I'm not a pro," she admitted. "But I've built things... small things."

Orin studied her avatar. "If you're willing to try, we'll compensate you. The district council pays freelancers in our governance token. It's not worth much now, but if the city recovers... it could be valuable."

Talia swallowed nervously. She had never freelanced. Never rebuilt a city. But something inside her whispered: *Say yes.*

"I'll do it."

The next morning, she logged in early and walked through the broken Sky District. She took notes. She inspected damaged scripts. She rebuilt cloud-walkways piece by piece. She restored lantern paths and redesigned storefronts with new lighting. She repaired teleport pads and created interactive sky gardens to make the district feel alive again.

Every day, she learned something new—design tricks, optimization secrets, scripting shortcuts. The more she fixed, the more the district revived. Visitors returned. Shops reopened. Musicians came back to perform. And with every improvement, the governance token she earned slowly increased in value.

One night, after weeks of work, Talia stood beneath the restored Sky Plaza—a huge floating platform surrounded by crystal archways. Hundreds of avatars had gathered to celebrate the district's reopening. Fireworks burst across the digital sky.

Orin approached her, smiling. "You saved Sky District."

Talia shook her head. "I just repaired a few things."

"You rebuilt an entire zone," Orin said. "And you did it beautifully."

Talia looked around. The glowing city felt different now—not just a place she visited, but a place she had shaped.

"People are asking about you," Orin continued. "Other districts want your help. There are jobs waiting—world builds, script repairs, event staging. Your portfolio here is incredible."

Talia's eyes widened. "My... portfolio?"

Orin nodded. "You're a freelancer now. One of the best we've seen."

It felt surreal. She had gone from a quiet employee stuck in a dull job to a creator trusted to craft digital worlds. Her tokens—once nearly worthless—were now worth more than her monthly paycheck. Her work attracted attention from DAOs, creators, and even small metaverse studios.

A month later, Talia quit her job—not out of frustration, but out of possibility. She rebuilt worlds full-time, designing floating temples, cyberpunk train stations, underwater spas, and magical academies. Her reputation soared. Clients sought her out. She earned more than she ever dreamed.

One evening, as she stood on a balcony overlooking the glowing clouds of Sky District—the world she had revived—Talia whispered to herself, "I rebuilt a sky."

But she hadn't just rebuilt a virtual city.

She had rebuilt her life.

The metaverse had given her something she never found in the real world: a chance to rewrite her story, one digital world at a time.

Chapter 10

Scaling Your Metaverse Empire for Long-Term Wealth

Building income streams in the metaverse is only the beginning. The real financial transformation occurs when you learn how to **scale** those income streams into a long-term digital empire. Scaling means multiplying your reach, automating your operations, expanding across platforms, diversifying revenue sources, and positioning your brand to continue earning whether you're online or not. The metaverse is built for scale because it removes traditional limitations—inventory, physical presence, geography, time zones, staff, and cost barriers. When you combine creativity with automation, strategic partnerships, and expansion, your metaverse income can grow far beyond anything a single-world creator could achieve.

The first step in scaling is **expanding across multiple metaverse platforms**. If you currently build in Decentraland, explore The Sandbox. If you sell wearables in Roblox, build cross-platform versions for other worlds. If you host events in Spatial, launch a parallel version in Meta Horizon. Every world has its own user base, economy, culture, and trends. By expanding across worlds, you increase visibility and tap into entirely new communities. Cross-platform branding multiplies your exposure, giving you more buyers, clients, collaborators, and opportunities. Worlds may rise or fall over time, but a cross-platform presence ensures your brand remains relevant and diversified.

The next step is **automation**. The metaverse allows you to automate nearly every business operation using scripts, bots, AI assistants, smart contracts, and automated marketplaces. You can automate royalty collection, wearable sales, NFT drops, event registration, onboarding flows, customer support, merchandise distribution, and recurring membership benefits. Automation reduces your workload while increasing your earning capacity. You can create systems that operate continuously—selling while you sleep, scaling without your presence, and building long-term passive income. The most successful metaverse entrepreneurs automate early and often.

Another key strategy is **hiring and delegation**. At some point, your brand will grow beyond what you can manage alone. You may need builders, scripters, designers, editors, community managers, marketers, or event staff. The metaverse allows you to hire talent from anywhere in the world. Freelancers can help you complete projects faster and maintain quality as you take on bigger clients or expand your portfolio. Delegation frees your time to focus on high-value work—strategy, branding, expansion, and partnerships.

Scaling also requires **partnerships**. Collaborate with artists, musicians, fashion designers, influencers, DJ collectives, game studios, marketplaces, and brands. Partnerships expand your audience, give you new resources, and increase your brand's credibility. Many creators double their income by partnering with high-profile builders or communities. Joint projects, co-branded releases, sponsored events, and collaborative worlds offer exponential growth opportunities. The metaverse thrives on shared creativity—the more partnerships you build, the faster your empire expands.

Another essential scaling strategy is **creating recurring revenue models**. One-time sales are good. Recurring revenue is freedom. You can introduce subscriptions, memberships, exclusive clubs, VIP passes, land rental systems, recurring events, token-gated access, or automated yield mechanisms that pay you monthly. Many creators design NFT memberships that unlock perks, early access, or exclusive areas inside worlds. Some run ongoing courses, workshops, or mentorship programs. Others build clubs, guilds, or communities with monthly dues. Recurring revenue stabilizes your income and gives you predictable cash flow—even during market fluctuations.

To scale effectively, you must also build **strong intellectual property**. This includes your brand name, avatar identity, signature art style, world themes, character designs, storytelling, and product collections. IP allows you to launch comics, merchandise, animations, games, collaborations, or physical products based on your metaverse brand. Strong IP becomes the foundation of long-term growth. It creates a universe your fans can explore, support, and invest in. Some of the biggest metaverse creators today started with a single wearable or build—and eventually grew into full franchises.

Another powerful scaling strategy is **community empowerment**. The more you empower your community, the more your brand grows without you. You can build ambassador programs, leadership roles, community-driven events, contests, incentives, and DAO-like structures that allow fans to participate in your world's growth. A strong community becomes your marketing engine, your loyal customer base, your support network, and your advocates. When your community becomes invested in your success, your empire expands exponentially.

Finally, long-term wealth in the metaverse requires **balancing active income with passive assets**. Active income comes from freelancing, building worlds, designing wearables, or hosting events. Passive income comes from royalties, land rentals, automated sales, DAO rewards, and token staking. The goal is to shift increasingly toward passive income while using active income to expand your portfolio. Over time, your metaverse empire should run like a digital machine—producing income with minimal manual work.

Scaling a metaverse empire is not about growing fast; it is about growing strategically. The creators who dominate the future will be those who combine creativity with business intelligence, community engagement, and multi-world influence. The metaverse is still in its infancy—meaning the opportunities available today are only the beginning. With consistent effort, strategic expansion, and innovative thinking, you can build a metaverse empire that lasts for decades, generating wealth long after the foundations have been laid.

The Architect of the Seven Worlds

Ren Farris never planned to build an empire. She started as a small creator in a quiet metaverse world, designing simple avatar accessories and a tiny floating tea garden. But as others discovered her work, her reputation grew. She became known as "The Garden Architect," a creator whose worlds felt alive—overflowing with light, sound, color, and emotion. She loved creating spaces that made people feel something. But she never imagined how far her journey would go.

One day, Ren received a message from a well-known DJ collective. "We want you to build a world for our next concert," they wrote. "Something magical. Something no one has ever seen." Ren hesitated—she had never built something large-scale—but she said yes.

Weeks later, her world was ready: a floating concert island shaped like a crescent moon, with water that glowed turquoise and a sky that pulsed to the beat of the music. When the event launched, thousands of avatars arrived. Screenshots went viral. Influencers praised her creativity. Brands reached out. Suddenly, Ren wasn't just a small creator—she was in demand.

But demand soon became overwhelming. Clients messaged her constantly. Requests piled up. She found herself working late into the night, unable to keep up. One evening, exhausted, she sat alone in her tea garden and whispered, "I can't do this alone."

A gentle voice responded. It was Nara, a builder she befriended months earlier. "Then don't," Nara said. "Build a team. Build a world that grows with you."

Ren realized she didn't need to shrink her dreams—she needed to expand her approach.

She hired her first assistant. Then a lighting designer. Then a world scripter. Then a community manager. Her small studio became a collective of talented creators from around the world. They called themselves **The Seven Lights**, inspired by the seven glowing lanterns that lit Ren's tea garden.

With her new team, Ren began expanding into other metaverse platforms. She recreated her tea garden in Spatial. She built a neon meditation pod in Horizon Worlds. She launched a cyberpunk sky café in Roblox. Each world had its own community—and each community embraced her work wholeheartedly.

As her influence grew, a DAO approached her with an offer. "We want you to design the central hub for our new decentralized city," they said. "In exchange, you'll receive governance tokens and revenue share from future events."

Ren accepted, unsure of what to expect. Months later, her design became the beating heart of an emerging digital civilization. She earned passive income from events, marketplaces, and tourism. Her tokens increased in value as the city expanded.

Her empire was no longer a dream—it was happening.

Ren then launched a **creator academy**, offering monthly workshops to teach new builders how to design worlds, create environments, and build immersive experiences. Hundreds joined. Some became freelancers. Others joined her studio. She realized she wasn't just building worlds—she was building careers.

Her community grew so large that members begged for an exclusive club. Ren created the **Garden of Seven Worlds**, a cross-platform membership where holders gained access to hidden gardens, private events, wearable drops, and collaborative builds. The membership sold out in minutes.

One night, after returning from a major event, Ren stood alone in her original tea garden—the tiny world where it all began. She listened to the wind chimes, watched the lanterns sway, and felt a quiet sense of awe. Nara appeared beside her.

"You built something extraordinary," Nara said.

Ren shook her head. "We built something extraordinary."

She looked out at the lantern-lit sky and realized every world she created, every team member she hired, every partnership she formed, and every community she nurtured had become part of a growing empire—an empire built not with borders and armies, but with creativity, collaboration, and imagination.

In seven different metaverse worlds, her creations stood like glowing monuments. And Ren knew her journey was far from over.

She was no longer just a builder.

She had become the **Architect of the Seven Worlds**—a creator whose empire would continue growing long after she logged out.

Epilogue

A Vision of Your Metaverse Future

The metaverse is still in its early childhood. Most people on Earth have never set foot inside a virtual world, never attended a digital concert, never purchased a wearable, never worked a Web3 job, and never invested in a virtual economy. Yet the foundations are already rising, and the creators, builders, entrepreneurs, and explorers who understand this new landscape early are positioning themselves for extraordinary long-term success. The metaverse is not a game—it is a new frontier, a new economy, and a new version of the internet where ownership, identity, creativity, and commerce merge into a unified digital universe. Those who learn how to harness its power now will stand among the pioneers shaping the future.

Throughout this audiobook, you learned the foundations of earning money inside virtual worlds—buying land, selling digital goods, hosting events, building communities, freelancing, investing in tokens, collaborating with brands, creating experiences, and scaling into a multi-world digital empire. But the true transformation happens when you realize that you are not simply participating in the metaverse—you are helping build it. Every world you design, every wearable you mint, every event you host, every DAO vote you cast, every item you sell, and every connection you form contributes to the evolution of this new digital civilization. The metaverse is not a single platform; it is a network of interconnected worlds where you can build anything you imagine without the limitations of the physical world.

The epilogue serves as a reminder that your metaverse journey is not ending—it is beginning. The skills you gained in this book are evergreen and will evolve as technology expands. Virtual reality, augmented reality, AI world-building tools, spatial computing, holo-projection, blockchain interoperability, and cross-platform avatars will continue reshaping the landscape. The metaverse will grow more immersive, more intuitive, and more integrated with everyday life. By mastering the foundations early, you will be prepared to ride every wave of innovation. Future careers that haven't been invented yet will emerge. New opportunities will appear in virtual education, remote collaboration hubs, AI-driven entertainment, digital real estate development, NFT-based employment, and immersive storytelling. You are not simply gaining skills—you are preparing for the next digital revolution.

The future belongs to creators who take action. You now understand that the metaverse rewards curiosity, consistency, experimentation, generosity, and creativity. Anyone can enter. Anyone can succeed. You don't need advanced tech skills, coding knowledge, or large investments. You need imagination and the willingness to learn. The first world you build may feel simple. Your first wearable may feel imperfect. Your first event may feel small. But the metaverse celebrates evolution, not perfection. Every creator who now dominates a platform started with something humble. With each creation, you grow stronger and more confident. You refine your style. You attract opportunities. You build community. You begin crafting your digital destiny.

As you move forward, remember the importance of community. The metaverse thrives on connection. People support the creators who show up, share value, contribute, collaborate, and uplift others. Your relationships will shape your success more than your tools. The creators who collaborate rise faster than those who isolate themselves. Join worlds, attend events, meet builders, join DAOs, participate in discussions, find mentors, and become a mentor yourself. The metaverse is more than a marketplace; it is a living, breathing society built on creativity and shared experiences. When you contribute to that society, it contributes back to you.

The final message of this epilogue is simple: **you are early**. You are entering the metaverse at a moment when the rules are still being written, the boundaries are still expanding, and the leaders of tomorrow are still learning today. You have the rare advantage of time—time to build, time to explore, time to establish yourself before the masses arrive. The creators who start now will become the authors of this new digital world. They will become the architects, teachers, entrepreneurs, entertainers, explorers, investors, and innovators that future generations study and follow.

There will never be a moment like this again—where the future of the internet is still forming, still flexible, still ripe with opportunity. You now have the knowledge, the strategies, and the vision to build something extraordinary inside the metaverse. Whether you choose to create worlds, design wearables, teach classes, run events, start a business, invest in DAOs, or build communities, the metaverse will reward your effort. And as your creations spread across digital universes, you become more than a participant—you become a pioneer shaping the future of human connection.

Your journey is just beginning. Continue building, continue dreaming, and continue expanding into the limitless frontier of Web3. The metaverse is waiting for you—and your empire has only just taken its first breath.

www.ingramcontent.com/pod-product-compliance
Ingram Content Group UK Ltd.
Pitfield, Milton Keynes, MK11 3LW, UK
UKHW020158290926
15471UKWH00005B/939

9 798295 491153